FACT or PHONY?

YOU SWALLOW SPIDERS IN YOUR SLEEP!

The Fact or Fiction Behind ANIMALS

PAUL MASON

Gareth Stevens
PUBLISHING

Please visit our website, **www.garethstevens.com**.
For a free color catalog of all our high-quality books,
call toll free 1-800-542-2595 or fax 1-877-542-2596.

Cataloging-in-Publication Data
Mason, Paul.
The fact or fiction behind animals / by Paul Mason.
p. cm. — (Fact or phony?)
Includes index.
ISBN 978-1-4824-4276-2 (library binding)
1. Animals — Miscellanea — Juvenile literature.
2. Common fallacies — Juvenile literature.
I. Mason, Paul, 1967-. II. Title.
QL49.M37 2016
590—d23

Published in 2016 by
Gareth Stevens Publishing
111 East 14th Street, Suite 349
New York, NY 10003

Editor: Debbie Foy
Design: Rocket Design (East Anglia) Ltd
Illustration: Alan Irvine

All illustrations by Shutterstock, except 4, 11, 20, 21, 27,
30-31, 37, 42, 65, 70 and 91.

Printed in the United States of America
CPSIA compliance information: Batch CW16GS: For further information contact Gareth Stevens, New York, New York at 1-800-542-2595.

HOW THIS BOOK CAN SAVE YOUR LIFE AND OTHER GOOD THINGS...

read on!

Read this part first...!

Most of us love animals — and people you meet are often full of information about them. You hear — or read on the Internet, or in emails — all kinds of crazy things:

"Avoid a shark attack by keeping as still as possible."

"Giant alligators live in the sewers."

"Earwigs can crawl into your ears and eat your brain."

Ahhhh, this is the life...

Are *any* of these actually true? Knowing whether they are or not could one day save your life. There's lots of advice out there on how to avoid being mauled by bears, gnawed by great white sharks, or battered by bulls, for example. Armed with a copy of this book you'll know which bits of advice are true, and which can be ignored.

Of course, this book won't only tell you about the animal myths that affect your safety. It will also stop you from looking like a complete idiot when someone confidently tells you something that sounds like fiction... but might just not be. Do you know for sure whether head lice prefer clean hair, whether ostriches bury their heads in the sand when scared, if all dogs are really wolves, or whether female praying mantises bite the heads off their boyfriends?

Finally, there are lots of sayings involving animals that are used to describe human behavior. People say things such as:

"YOU CAN'T TEACH AN OLD DOG NEW TRICKS."

"OH YES – AND PIGS MIGHT FLY."

"IT WAS LIKE A RED RAG TO A BULL."

"AN ELEPHANT NEVER FORGETS."

These sayings have been handed down through the years, without anyone really knowing whether or not they're true. But have no fear, **FACT OR PHONY** will reveal the truth: are bulls *honestly* enraged by the color red? Have pigs ever flown? Do elephants really have good memories? And much, much more...

read on!

Crocodiles cry while they eat you!

Ever heard the expression "crocodile tears"? It means fake tears, cried when the person doesn't really feel sad at all. Like when your little sister or brother starts crying after they break your tablet, hoping for sympathy.

The expression "crocodile tears" comes from an old, old legend. People say that as a crocodile bites its victim, tears spring from its eyes. It's as if the croc is sad about having to make a meal of another living creature.

★ And the truth is...

Crocodiles can't really chew, so they have to bite off chunks of their prey (an arm or a leg, perhaps) and swallow it whole. As the big lump of meat is gulped down the crocodile's throat, it presses on the glands that keep the croc's eyes moist. This forces tears to pop out of its eyes.

Verdict: _____ FACT _____

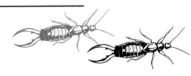

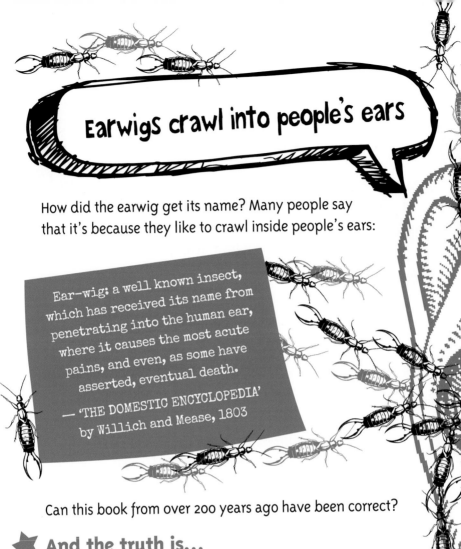

Earwigs crawl into people's ears

How did the earwig get its name? Many people say that it's because they like to crawl inside people's ears:

> Ear-wig: a well known insect, which has received its name from penetrating into the human ear, where it causes the most acute pains, and even, as some have asserted, eventual death.
>
> — 'THE DOMESTIC ENCYCLOPEDIA' by Willich and Mease, 1803

Can this book from over 200 years ago have been correct?

 And the truth is...

Earwigs do like to hide themselves in warm, moist places — but not in human ears. Even if one did crawl in, there's a bone across your ear canal that would stop it from getting very far.

People actually think earwigs got their name from the way their fully extended wings look like human ears.

Verdict:  **PHONY**

You can't teach an old dog new tricks

This is a phrase you hear in all sorts of situations. For example:

★ *Your dad decides to take up skateboarding, falls over, and breaks his wrist*

★ *Your grandma goes to belly-dancing classes, where her sweatpants elastic breaks and she makes a fool of herself*

★ *Your geography teacher decides to start a lunchtime hip-hop club with hideously embarrassing results.*

"Well," people will say, "you can't teach an old dog new tricks." But are they right?

★ The truth is...

All it takes is a bit of dedication from their owner, and a dog of any age can learn new tricks. Fifteen minutes or so a day should be enough to get even the most senior doggie citizens sitting, staying, lying down, or just about anything else-ing.

Verdict: with enough time and doggy treats...

 5 things you (probably) didn't know about CATS

1 Cats can squeeze through any space wide enough for their whiskers.

2 Only cats, giraffes, and camels walk using both left legs, then both right legs.

3 Cats can make ten times as many noises as dogs.

4 Strangely, cats are unable to taste sweet food.

5 If you put a cat on a vegetarian diet, it will die.

GIANT ALLIGATORS LURK IN NEW YORK'S SEWERS

Every once in a while, an *actual* alligator of some sort pops up on the streets of New York City. In just the last few years:

> A small caiman* was caught wandering around among the picnicking families in Central Park. It had been living in one of the lakes.

> Another caiman was captured by the cops outside an apartment building in Brooklyn, after hissing and snapping at them in an effort to resist arrest.

> An alligator was spotted lurking under a parked car in Queens, only to be scooped up by the long arm of the law.

All these reptiles were small, less than 3 feet (1 m) long. But stories suggest that down in the sewers, far bigger monsters may be lurking.

Stories about alligators in New York's sewers have been around for nearly 100 years. In the 1930s a former city official called Teddy May told of having seen colonies of alligators — some of them huge — living in the sewers.

A smaller, slimmer relative of the alligator, originally from Central or South America.

Where did these alligators come from? The story goes that people who had visited Florida brought them to the city as pets. But the alligators grew, as alligators do. They were either let go at night or, if small enough, flushed down the toilet.

Once down in the sewers the alligators thrived. They grew bigger and bigger, met other alligators, had babies, and generally took over. Pretty soon it was a brave sewer worker who went into the darkest, deepest parts of the system.

Ahhhh, this is the life...

★ And the truth is...

Oddly, in 1935 a 7.2-foot (2.5 m) alligator *was* caught in the sewers. It can't have been living there for long, though — alligators are cold-blooded and need warmth to survive, but New York's sewers are freezing in winter. Also, an alligator would probably find it impossible to survive the pollution down there.

Verdict: —— PHONY ——

WHEN ANIMALS ATTACK!

ESCAPING A BEAR

Think what it must be like for the bear. Every year, noisy hikers visit their woods and disturb the peace. The only thing worse is the smell of delicious food the hikers trail around after themselves. No wonder bears sometimes forget their manners and attack humans.

How can you stop it from happening to you?

★ If the bear is 330 feet (100 m) or more away but has spotted you, start talking loudly but calmly. Once it realizes you're human, it will probably run.

★ If it gets aggressive, don't run — you won't escape. Instead try to back slowly away, without looking the bear in the eye.

★ Climbing a tree may show the bear that you're not threatening it — but bears can climb trees too, so this won't be an escape.

Head lice prefer clean hair

Sometimes, it seems you just can't win. You try to keep yourself looking clean and tidy, washing your hair every day. Then someone comes along and says:

"You know head lice prefer clean hair, don't you? You're making it more likely you'll catch them."

In a way, this makes perfect sense. After all, if you were a head louse, where would you prefer to live? In a dirty, greasy forest of hair — or a lovely, clean, sweet-smelling one?

 But the truth is...

Head lice set up home on your head in order to drink your blood. They have a mouth like a tiny sharp-ended straw, which they stick into your scalp and suck through. They clasp onto your hair near the skin, but they can clasp on to clean hair or dirty hair equally well — it doesn't make any difference to them!

Verdict: —— PHONY ——

13

An elephant never forgets

There's actually a much earlier version of this saying, from ancient Greece: "A camel never forgets an injury." Today people say it's elephants that never forget, or that people with a good memory have "a memory like an elephant."

This idea is probably based on the fact that elephants have the biggest brain of any land animal. With all that brain, they must be using it for something, right? Surely little details like their phone number or mom's birthday couldn't get lost in there?

★ **And the truth is...**
Elephants are able to remember every detail of their home territory, especially things like where to find water, food, or somewhere good to have a bath. They also remember the faces of other elephants. Years after seeing another elephant, they are able to recognize old friends immediately.

Verdict:

Cheetahs are the world's fastest animals

Grown-ups love this fact, and will bring it up again and again. The cheetah can run at about 68 mph (110 kph), which is pretty fast. It would be able to keep up in the fast lane of the highway (though not quite fast enough to get a speeding ticket). Cheetahs can only keep at maximum speed for about 30 seconds — after that, they overheat and have to slow down.

And the truth is...

Cheetahs are fast, but not the fastest. The peregrine falcon reaches speeds of about 200 mph (320 kph) as it dives down — or "stoops" — after its prey. Of course, you might say that's cheeting (ha!), because the falcon has gravity helping it. But another bird, the spine-tailed swift, can fly at about 108 mph (175 kph) without help from gravity. That's plenty fast enough for a speeding ticket!

The cheetah is, though, the fastest land animal.

Verdict: a bit true, but mostly

> ## Peeing on a jellyfish sting will cure it

There are few things worse than going for a lovely swim on a hot day, then being stung by a jellyfish. (Seeing a shark's fin appear alongside you is one of them — see pages 32-33 for ideas on how to get out of *that* situation.)

A jellyfish sting happens when you brush against its tentacles. These are armed with stingers, which pierce your skin and inject venom. The pain happens right away, and can be very bad.

Someone's bound to tell you that the cure for the sting is for someone to pee on it. But even if the pain's so bad you're tempted to agree — will it work?

★ The truth is...

Pee won't help, and could make it worse. The chemical makeup of pee will probably cause the stingers left on your skin to release more venom. For most stings, the best treatment is to wash it down with seawater.

Verdict:  PHONY

16

⭐ 5 things you (probably) didn't know about CAMELS

1 Camels can't live without water for as long as giraffes ...

2 ... or rats.

3 Camels like company, which is why they hang out in herds.

4 When they are angry, scared, or frustrated, camels spit. The rotten juice they gob at you comes up from their stomach.

5 Camels have the biggest mouths of any ruminants*, so they can give a nasty bite.

*Hoofed mammals that chew mainly grass, and have several chambers in their stomach

You can make two worms by cutting one in half

Anyone who's ever done any gardening will have consoled themselves with this myth under their breath — usually just a few moments after accidentally chopping a worm in half.

Worms do, in fact, continue to wriggle around after they've been chopped in half. This is probably what started the idea going in the first place. That, and the fact that no one can tell one end of a worm from another. Worms look the same at both ends, so it stands to reason that if you chop one in half, both ends will carry on doing their wormy thing. Doesn't it?

★ The truth is...

Why do those worms keep wriggling after being chopped? They're busy dying, and the wriggles are actually death throes.

The head end just might survive, if only a little bit of the tail has been cut off — but the tail end definitely dies.

Verdict: ─── a teeny bit true, but mostly  **PHONY**

Pigs can't fly

"Oh yes — and pigs might fly" is a common way of saying something could never happen. The idea of a pig taking to the skies is pretty strange. They lack many of the things traditionally needed for flight: wings, jet engines, plane tickets, etc.

 But the truth is...

In 1703, England was hit by one of the most terrible storms ever seen. About 15,000 people were killed, mainly by flying debris. And in there among the flying debris were chickens, sheep, and — you guessed it — pigs. They had all been picked up off the ground by the wind.

Pigs are very intelligent animals. They must have been wondering if the old saying about their not being able to fly was actually wrong — just before they hit the ground with a conclusive thump.

Verdict:  **FACT**

I'D NEVER HAVE KNOWN...

... that lobsters can live as long as humans

Lobsters grow slowly, and can live a very long time. Most of the lobsters people eat are about 20 years old, but there are some real old giants crawling around on the seabed.

The oldest lobsters are probably over 100 years old, and weigh about the same as a medium-sized dog.

Speaking of which, the French poet Gérard de Nerval had a pet lobster called Thibault. He used to take it for walks around Paris!

one dog year equals seven human ones

People will often tell you that to figure out how old a dog is in human terms, you should multiply its age by seven. So, a 3-year-old poodle would be 21 in human terms. A 9-year-old Labrador would be 63, and just thinking about retirement.

 ## And the truth is...

This myth is based on the idea that dogs live one-seventh as long as humans — about 11 years. Bigger pedigree dogs, such as Labradors and Alsatians, do live about this long. Smaller dogs and non-pedigrees usually live longer, and many make it to 15 years or more. Using the seven-year rule, a 15-year-old dog would be 105 in human years.

Verdict: ——— mostly

Headless chickens

Admittedly they can't run very well. The phrase "running around like a chicken with its head cut off" is used to describe someone who flaps about aimlessly, without getting anything done. But can chickens *really* keep racing around the yard, after their heads have been chopped off?

 ## The truth is...

Just before the chicken's head is chopped off, it realizes something is going badly wrong in its life. First it is chased around and grabbed. Then a chopping block and a large ax come into view.

All this excitement releases a hormone called adrenaline into the chicken's muscles. Adrenaline stimulates muscle activity, so even after the chicken's head has been chopped off, the muscles keep on twitching. Sometimes the bird's wings flap enough to move it along the ground as though it's running.

Verdict: just about

can still run around

THE STRANGE CASE OF MIKE

Headless chickens may be able to flap around for a few seconds after their heads have been chopped off, but this activity is usually over after 30 seconds or less. How about the reports of a chicken that survived for a year and a half without a head?

The chicken was actually a cockerel called Mike. His owner chopped off his head one morning in 1945. By late afternoon, Mike was still strutting around the farmyard (although without his head, so he must have found it extremely hard not to bang into things).

Mike's owner poured some food down his neck (literally), and took him on tour. The headless chicken lasted another 18 months, and earned lots of money, before his owner forgot to clear out his breathing hole one evening. Sadly, poor old Mike choked to death.

HOWDY!

 And the truth?
All true. When his head was chopped off, enough of Mike's brain stem was left for him to carry on living. He probably didn't even notice that his head was missing.

FACT

Verdict: _____

I'D NEVER HAVE KNOWN...

... that foxes are better than cats at catching mice

Rodents such as mice make a tasty snack for a hungry fox — and they have a brilliant technique for catching them.

The fox leaps up in the air (up to about 3 feet, or 1 m), and comes down vertically towards the mouse. Either:

a The mouse jumps upwards, straight into the fox's mouth, or;

b The fox uses its paws to pin the mouse down, stunning it and enabling the fox to sink its teeth in!

The box jellyfish is the world's deadliest killer

The box jellyfish is a small, near-invisible creature that floats into shore dragging its deadly tentacles behind it. Every year swimmers accidentally brush against these tentacles and are injected with powerful venom.

Those who are badly stung die a painful death. The venom attacks their skin, heart, and nervous system. Swimmers may die of shock, a heart attack or drowning before they can even reach the shore. It's no wonder the box jellyfish is sometimes said to be the world's deadliest killer.

 ## But the truth is...

Box jellyfish kill several people each year. But lots of animals are equally, if not more, deadly to humans. The saltwater crocodile, Indian cobra, hippopotamus, great white shark, Brazilian wandering spider, and Cape buffalo claim thousands of victims each year.

The deadliest living animal is the mosquito — or to be exact, the female Anopheles mosquito. When these critters bite, they spread malaria and other awful diseases, which kill over a million people a year.

Verdict:

YOU SHOULD SUCK VENOM OUT OF SNAKEBITES

At one time, scenes based on this idea appeared in just about every adventure movie/Western/war film. At some point, a snake would bite somebody. Usually it was a rattlesnake, but sometimes a black mamba. (This is one of the world's deadliest snakes, able to kill a grown elephant — or several humans — with its venom.)

In the movies, when someone is bitten by a snake the following procedure has to be followed:

1. Tie a tourniquet around the leg that's been bitten.

2. Slice the bite open with a knife.

3. Suck out the venom into your mouth

4. Spit it out.

5. Rinse out your mouth with water; spit again; say, "He'll be OK now" as the victim falls backwards with relief.

So, if you happen to be bitten by a venomous* snake, would this be a good way to react?

*Venoms are harmful when injected into your flesh; poisons are harmful if swallowed or breathed in. That's why biting snakes are called "venomous," and why in theory it would be safe to suck venom out of a bite.

⭐ The truth is...

You are unlikely to be able to suck any venom from the snakebite. Trying it is not likely to do you any harm — but if there are cuts inside your mouth, the venom could enter your body through these.

The best treatment for snakebite is to keep the victim calm and still, which stops their heart from beating fast and spreading the venom quickly round their body. Call the emergency services as soon as possible.

Verdict:  **PHONY**

> ## Turkeys are so stupid, they sometimes look up at falling rain until they drown

The full version of this is that domesticated turkeys have had all their natural intelligence bred out of them. In fact, they're so stupid that when they first feel a drop or two of rain, they look up at the sky, open-mouthed in fascination. Their mouths fill with rainwater, and they drown.

★ The truth is...

Domesticated turkeys are often thought to lack intelligence — but the idea of them being fascinated by rain is wrong. They would either look for shelter, or carry on with what they were doing.

In addition, turkeys have eyes on the sides, not the front, of their head. So they wouldn't look up to see rain, they would turn their head sideways.

Verdict: PHONY

☆ 5 things you (probably) didn't know about CROCODILES

1 Crocodiles can run at speeds of up to 10.5 mph (17 kph), but only for short distances. However …

2 … they can launch themselves out of the water at speeds of up to 25 mph (40 kph).

3 A crocodile's bite is 12 times more powerful than a great white shark's.

4 Crocodiles have very weak jaw-opening muscles. It's possible to tape their jaws shut with packing tape.

5 The bigger the pool, the bigger the croc it will hold. Crocodiles never outgrow the pool in which they live.

TIGERS HAVE

This sounds unlikely, doesn't it? Everyone knows tigers have stripy fur, not skin. That's what makes a tiger a tiger, after all. Whether it's a Siberian tiger, a Bengal tiger, a Sumatran tiger, or some other kind, they all have stripy fur.

STRIPY SKIN

⭐ **The truth is...**

It would have been a brave person who first shaved a live tiger to discover this, but a tiger's pattern of black stripes is indeed contained on its skin, as well as its fur.

FACT

Verdict: _____

WHEN ANIMALS ATTACK!

So, you're out for a swim and you see the thing everyone dreads — a fin rising up and starting to circle you. The music from Jaws starts up in your head — duuh dun... duuh dun... dun dun, dun dun, dundun, dundun, dundundundundundundundun.

How do you avoid becoming a great white lunch?

★ Keep the shark in sight. Your best chance of surviving is to beat off the attack, if it comes.

★ Shout, or wave your arms over your head, to attract help from nearby boats or the shore.

ESCAPING A GREAT WHITE SHARK

★ Great whites like to attack into the sun. If the shark disappears, it is likely to emerge from below towards the sun shining on the surface. Check beneath you!

★ Fight back if the shark comes close enough — attack its eyes and gills, as this may force it to think again.

You swallow spiders in your sleep!

And what's more, we apparently swallow eight spiders a year.

Few people are loony enough to pick up a spider and gulp it down while they're awake. The idea is that as you lie there drooling on your pillow, spiders can approach and crawl in. Three main reasons for the spiders' attraction to the mouths of sleeping humans have been put forward:

1 **One report says that spiders are attracted by the smell of rotten food between your teeth (if true, this is a very good reason to floss regularly!).**

2 **Others suggest that the vibrations of people snoring have a fatal attraction for spiders.**

3 Some people think the spiders are just looking for a quiet place to rest. This does rather disagree with the snoring theory, but never mind… zzzzz.

⭐ And the facts are…

Just thinking about this for a few seconds shows how unlikely it is to be true. Why on earth would a spider deliberately climb into someone's mouth? Spiders don't live in people's mouths. Even though they don't have very big brains, spiders can presumably tell that a mouth is not a comfortable resting place.

This entire story is a hoax. It was dreamed up and circulated (along with a bunch of other unbelievable stories) in 1993. Within months it had spread across the world by email, ending up being reported as fact in several newspapers.

Verdict: ——— **PHONY**

⭐ 5 things you (probably) didn't know about DOGS

1 The tallest dog was a Great Dane who was 41 inches (104 cm) high at the shoulder.

2 The smallest recorded dog was a 2.5-inch (6.35 cm) Yorkshire terrier.

3 Louis Doberman, a German tax collector, developed the Doberman breed. He wanted fierce, strong dogs to protect him while he collected money from people!

4 When their dog died, grief-stricken ancient Egyptians are said to have shaved off their own eyebrows and smeared their hair with mud.

5 A dog's noseprint is as unique as a human fingerprint.

WHEN ANIMALS TELL THE TIME

Many dog owners say that their pet always knows when it's time to be fed. They sit waiting by their bowl or gaze at their owner.

Dogs don't actually check their watches when it's time for dinner, but they do know that when they feel this hungry, they usually get fed. So they sit waiting by their bowl for dinner to arrive!

Ostriches bury their heads in the sand

The full version of this is that when scared or threatened, ostriches will quickly bury their heads in the sand. It's a birdy version of what little kids sometimes do; they cover their eyes with their hands and shout:

"You can't see me!"

If it's true, it proves that ostriches are remarkably stupid, and makes you wonder how on earth they've managed to survive for so long.

⭐ And the truth is...

Ostriches do put their heads in holes in the sand — but not because they're scared. They dig holes in the dirt to lay their eggs, and regularly lean down into the hole to turn the eggs with their beaks. From a distance, it can look as though they're burying their heads in the sand.

Verdict:  PHONY

Touching a toad gives you warts

When you think of witches do you think of bubbling cauldrons? Black cats and broomsticks? Toads hopping and leaping everywhere? Warty noses?

Maybe it's this image of warty witches that gives us the idea that touching a toad will give you warts. Or maybe it's the way toads look. Their skin is often covered in lumps and bumps that look like warts. Since the toads are covered in warty growths, and warts are infectious, it's obvious that if you touch a toad you'll get warts. Isn't it?

 And the truth is...

Toads aren't covered in warts. The lumps on their skin are glands, which release mucus or poison when the toad is alarmed or threatened.

We get warts from a virus, called HPV. The H stands for "human" — showing that the virus is a human one... not a toad one.

Verdict:

WHEN ANIMALS ATTACK!

ESCAPING A CROCODILE

It's a beautiful warm evening, you're on vacation — why not take a walk down by that tropical river? BECAUSE IT'S FULL OF CROCODILES!

Here's how to avoid becoming a croco-dinner:

 Don't swim or wade in areas where crocodiles are found. Sounds obvious, but each year many people are killed by crocs while doing just that.

 Crocodiles are terrible at running from side to side, so if one chases you, run in zigzags.

 Stay away from the water's edge, and always face the water — they wait till your back's turned to attack.

 Don't visit the same spot day after day — one day, there will be a croc waiting for you.

You can hypnotize an alligator

This story goes that if you know what you're doing, you can put an alligator into a hypnotic trance. This renders it helpless and unable to move.

Florida's Seminole Indians are said to have discovered this trick. They would hold the alligator's mouth shut — which is easy, because they have very weak jaw-opening muscles. Then they would roll the alligator on its back with its tail held still, and its belly was stroked. The alligator would go into a trance, and would only wake up when someone touched it.

⭐ And the truth is...

This can be done, and not only on alligators. Some sharks have been put into a similar trance-like state, for example. (Don't try and fight off a shark attack by tickling its tummy, though!)

Verdict:

I'D NEVER HAVE KNOWN...

... that donkeys aren't scared of lions

Well, perhaps that's a bit of an exaggeration. But donkeys are the only animals of their size that will face up to a lion, rather than running away.

That's why in Africa, brave (if a bit crazy) donkeys are sometimes used to guard herds of cattle against attacks by lions.

Lemmings throw themselves off cliffs

The full story goes that groups of lemmings regularly commit mass suicide by throwing themselves off cliffs or into rivers. (If you've never met a lemming, it's a small furry rodent.) This is said to show:

a) That lemmings are really stupid, and;

b) That a lemming will follow the lemming in front of it almost anywhere.

"You're behaving like a lemming" is a way of telling someone you think they're following blindly along the road to disaster.

 The truth is...

When there's lots of food around, lemming populations grow very fast. (A female lemming can produce 80 young in just one year.) Soon, the lemmings eat all the food nearby, and have to move on. Usually they just find a new place and start eating again — but once in a while, the plan goes wrong. The lemmings hit a cliff or a river and, being not-that-intelligent, plop over it. But they're not committing suicide; they're just making a mistake.

Verdict: a bit true, but mostly  PHONY

All dogs have a bit of wolf in them

It's easy to believe that an Alsatian or a husky might be descended from wolves. But a Yorkshire terrier, or a Chihuahua? No way... surely not?

The truth is...

Incredibly, all dogs are descended from wolves — even Paris Hilton's Tinkerbell. No one knows how humans and wolves first got together. Maybe wolves started nosing around humans and got less and less nervous of them. Or maybe humans found some wolf cubs and decided to adopt them.

So, why don't all dogs look like wolves? It's because over the centuries (dogs have been alongside us for about 13,000 years), we've bred them for specific uses. For example, you wouldn't send a greyhound to catch rats, or a Jack Russell to run around a track.

Verdict: FACT

Hyenas are so nasty, they laugh when they've killed something

Most people who have seen hyenas instinctively fear them. They look like a kind of Frankenstein's dog. With their snarling faces, sloped backs and powerful shoulders they look like a cross between a cat and a wolf. And you're right to be scared. A quarter of all animals that are hunted as prey in Africa are killed by hyenas.

Hyenas are extremely aggressive. They're usually born as twins, but one twin often eats the other to show it who's boss (which certainly works). As adults, they can eat a third of their body weight in just half an hour.

Worst of all, hyenas are said to laugh as they eat into their victims (often before they're even dead).

 ## And the truth is...

Hyenas do laugh at a kill site — but not for joy. What sounds to us like a laugh is actually a weaker member of the hyena pack showing submission to a stronger one. He or she is saying, "Don't bite me — you eat first. I'll just wait till you've finished."

Verdict:

Cow farts are destroying the world

This myth is all about global warming. Global warming is caused by an increase in the number of greenhouse gases in the atmosphere. These gases trap heat, slowly increasing the world's temperature. This is causing all kinds of trouble: changes in our weather, a rise in sea levels, and an increase in natural disasters such as hurricanes.

But what's all that got to do with cows?

There are millions and millions of cows in the world, and they're constantly eating, which produces a lot of pee, poop, and farts. Unfortunately, cow farts contain the greenhouse gas methane — which is far worse for the environment than the most common greenhouse gas, carbon dioxide.

★ And the truth is...

Cow farts aren't destroying the world. It's their burps. They burp out loads of methane every day — some estimates say they constitute 4% of the world's greenhouse gas emissions! And because methane is so much more damaging than carbon dioxide, cow burps are having a really big effect.

Verdict: ————— the right idea, but actually  PHONY

✩ 5 things you (probably) didn't know about ELEPHANTS

1 Elephants are the only mammals that can't jump, but ...

2 ... they *can* stand on their heads — not too many animals can do that!

3 Elephants only sleep for two hours a day.

4 Elephants can't run, as it would damage their bones. Mind you, they can do a fast walk of 15.5 mph (25 kph).

5 Up to 9.5 quarts (9 l) of water can be held inside an elephant's trunk.

I'D NEVER HAVE KNOWN...

... dogs wag their tails when they're sad, as well as happy

If a dog is wagging its tail more to the right (the dog's right, not yours), it's expressing pleasure or excitement.

Dogs that wag their tails more to the left are showing nervousness or fear.

The hippopotamus is Africa's most dangerous animal

Africa is full of dangerous animals: deadly black mamba snakes*, giant Nile crocodiles, lions, leopards, etc, etc. But the most dangerous one might come as a surprise: it's the bumbling old hippopotamus.

Hippos aren't quite as harmless as they first seem. For a start, their mouths have huge teeth, up to 1.6 feet (0.5 m). They're easily capable of biting off a man's head as he cowers in a hole, trying to hide.

Get between a hippo and the water — especially if it's a mother hippo with young swimming around — and the adult hippo can be very aggressive. And males are always aggressive if you wander into their territory.

 And the facts are...

All true. You'll know if a hippo gets annoyed, because it will start to sweat red sticky stuff. Knowing it's annoyed probably won't do you much good, though — despite looking a bit hefty, hippos can run at over 18.6 mph (30 kph).

*See page 26 for a bit more about these.

Verdict:

POLAR NOSES

Polar bears are just about perfectly designed for hunting seals out on the Arctic ice. They're the largest land-based meat eater, and are armed with some pretty terrifying weapons:

⭐ *Huge feet up to 12 inches (30 cm) across support the bear's weight as it stalks its prey across the snow and ice. They are tipped with claws that can rip a seal's belly open.*

⭐ *An amazing sense of smell, which allows the bear to smell seals from 1 mile (1.6 km) away, and through 3.3 feet (1 m) of snow.*

⭐ *A top speed of 25 mph (40 kph).*

⭐ *Powerful jaws that can crush a seal's skull in one bite.*

There's just one problem for the polar bear. Its white coat is ideal camouflage for creeping up on seals — but its black nose isn't. That nose stands out like a cherry in the middle of a white-iced cake. So as the bears creep up on their prey, they apparently cover their noses with their paws.

50

BEARS COVER THEIR WHEN HUNTING

And the truth is...

The idea of polar bears covering their black noses for better disguise is often repeated. It appears in the myths of some Arctic native peoples, who use it to show what a careful and dangerous hunter the bear is. But despite the fact that many polar bears have their own film-crew entourages, no one has ever recorded a polar bear doing this.

Verdict:  **PHONY**

A few more (untrue) myths about polar bears:

1. All polar bears are left-handed.

2. Polar bears use tools to kill their prey (for example by throwing blocks of ice at them).

3. The only animal that hunts polar bears is the killer whale (actually, polar bears are a top predator: nothing hunts them except humans).

WHEN ANIMALS ATTACK!

ESCAPING A GORILLA

There you are, wandering through the African highlands one day. Suddenly, you come face to face with a giant male silverback gorilla — and he's not very happy to have been woken from his favorite afternoon nap.

If he starts hooting, then throwing plants (and possibly a bit of his own poop) at you, he's going into attack mode.

How do you avoid being torn limb from limb?

★ Don't look him in the eye — instead, look down at the ground and to one side.

★ Slowly back away, but without turning around until you can no longer see the grumpy giant.

★ If he does attack, your best hope — and it's not a very good one, to be honest — is to curl up into a ball and "play dead"!

Most shark attacks happen in water less than 3.3 feet (1 m) deep

If you've ever seen the film *Jaws*, you'll have a mental picture of a particular scene. The swimmer is in deep water, a long way from the beach, and the ocean is calm. Suddenly, a fin breaks the surface… a big fin.

Without being too gory, it's not a scene that ends well for the swimmer.

We all think that's how shark attacks happen: in deep water, far from the beach. In the shallows we're pretty safe. But then along comes this factoid: most shark attacks happen in less than 3 feet (1 m) of water. Argh! Can it be true?

 ## The fact is…

As a bare fact, this is true — but it's a bit misleading. When someone says "shark attack" we think of a person losing a limb, or even their life. Most shark attacks in shallow water are by small sharks that have bumped into someone. They bite to see what they've bumped into, then swim off. Most *deadly* shark attacks happen out past the surf line, in deeper water.*

*Don't worry, you're still more likely to die in a collapsing-sand-hole accident on the beach than in a shark attack.

Verdict: technically TRUE… but really,

53

Kangaroos are good at boxing

Boxing kangaroos are a symbol of Australian pride. During World War II they were painted as symbols on Australian fighter planes and ships. Today, the Australian Olympic team uses the boxing kangaroo image. But are kangaroos actually any good at boxing?

 The truth is...

In the late 1900s, traveling shows gave men the chance to box against kangaroos in the ring. The men rarely, if ever, won. Male kangaroos* box each other over females or access to drinking spots. They grapple with their smaller front paws, and make powerful kicks with their back paws.

*The name for a group of kangaroos is a "mob."

Verdict: —————————

No one knows where eels come from

For centuries, sailors would say that eels came from the mysterious Sargasso Sea, an open water sea in the Atlantic Ocean. It's the only sea in the world without a coastline. They might be right — in fact they probably are right — but then again, they might not be…

⭐ The truth is…

Young European freshwater eels are born far out to sea, then swim towards land. They swim up rivers, and live there for anything between 6 and 40 years, until they are ready to breed. Then they leave the river and return to the sea, swimming thousands of miles to… where?

Most scientists *think* eels breed in the Sargasso Sea, south of Bermuda. That's where the smallest baby eels ever captured have been found. But no one has actually seen baby eels being born there, or caught a ready-to-spawn female — so there's no definite proof.

Verdict: technically

⭐ 5 things you (probably) didn't know about SHARKS

1 There are no known diseases that affect sharks.

2 Sharks can keep on biting even if their own insides have been bitten out.

3 Sharks won't eat near the place where they've given birth ...

4 ... but they will eat anything, anywhere else.

5 Bull sharks — which regularly attack humans — can swim in both sea and freshwater.

Just a few of the things found in the stomachs of sharks:
★ a tom-tom drum ★ a chicken coop ★ a pair of shoes
★ a chair ★ an unexploded bomb.

When cows lie down, it's going to rain

This is an old bit of wisdom from before the days of hourly weather forecasts and satellite pictures on the internet. People used to say that if you spotted a bunch of cows lying down, it was a sure sign rain was on its way.

★ The truth is...

Cows usually lie down because they're chewing the cud. (Cud is food that has been chewed once already, then regurgitated to be chewed a second time. Yuck.) It doesn't have anything to do with the weather.

Verdict:  PHONY

More (incorrect) sayings about cows:

1. Cows listening to music will produce more milk.

2. If you cut a piece from a cow's tail, she will never run off.

3. Cows always lie down on Christmas Day.

I'D NEVER HAVE KNOWN...

... that ferrets can get depressed

Many of us think of ferrets as the smelly, violent thugs of the rodent world. It's not true — ferrets are actually very entertaining, and people have been keeping them as pets for at least 2,000 years.

Ferrets are extremely playful. When excited they "dance" sideways, twisting and jumping, while making soft hissing sounds or "chuckling." Some ferrets even do somersaults. But they also have a sensitive side. If they're separated from a companion, ferrets can fall into a depression. They don't want to play, they stop eating, and just lie around and sleep all day!

Lobsters scream when you cook them

Any chef will tell you that a lobster has to be eaten fresh. If you kill it and leave it lying around for a while, it will go bad. That's why seafood restaurants often have live lobsters wandering around in a tank, waiting to be cooked. (It's the kind of waiting room you never want to find yourself in!)

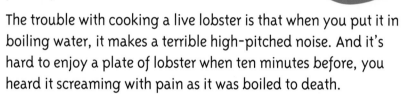

The trouble with cooking a live lobster is that when you put it in boiling water, it makes a terrible high-pitched noise. And it's hard to enjoy a plate of lobster when ten minutes before, you heard it screaming with pain as it was boiled to death.

 But the truth is...

No one knows for sure whether lobsters feel pain, but one thing *is* for sure: they can't scream. Lobsters don't have vocal cords or lungs like humans do, so it would be impossible for them. The noise they make when being cooked is just hot air escaping from their shells.

Verdict: PHONY

Cockroaches would survive a nuclear war

The idea behind this myth is that cockroaches would be the only living things to survive a nuclear war. Almost everyone has heard this said, and hardly anyone knows whether it's true or not.

★ The truth is...

Cockroaches are very tough: if there were to be a nuclear war, they'd survive a lot longer than humans. But the last creatures left alive would almost certainly be bacteria, which are very adaptable and can live almost anywhere.

Verdict: PHONY

Bulls get angry when they see the color red

The idea that bulls get furious whenever they see the color red is so common that it's even become a popular saying:

"Like a red rag to a bull."

It's used to describe something that's guaranteed to make a person angry. But do bulls really get mad and decide to attack whenever they see something red?

⭐ And the truth is...

Bulls aren't very good at spotting different colors. They *may* see red, but are quite likely to confuse it with green or blue. The color doesn't make them angry. People probably got the idea that it does because matadors at bullfights have red capes, which the bulls charge at. But the bull is likely to be angry because the matador is trying to stick a sword in its back, not because of the red cape.

Verdict: PHONY

WHEN ANIMALS ATTACK!

ESCAPING A BIG CAT

No, we don't mean that large Siamese from down the road — we mean cats like leopards, tigers and lions. They generally like to creep up on their prey from behind, but if you do spot one stalking you, how do you avoid becoming lunch?

★ Don't run away — this tells the cat you're prey, and it will attack.

★ Stare at it — in the cat world, this is a sign of aggression. Who knows, maybe it will back down?

★ Make yourself look as big as possible, and shout as loudly as you can without sounding panicky.

★ If an attack happens, fight back with a stick or rocks.

A lizard grows a new tail if the old one gets left behind

OK, by "left behind," we actually mean ripped off by a predator. There's a long-standing belief that if a lizard's tail is grabbed by an attacker, and it has a choice between:

a *Being eaten*

OR

b *Leaving its tail behind (as a sort of consolation prize/ distraction) and legging it to safety*

the lizard will choose option "b" every time.

Not only that — in a short space of time the lizard will have grown a brand-new tail, ready for the next great escape.

⭐ And the truth is...

One of the most common types of lizard is known as a skink. They're small creatures about 4 inches (10 cm) long. Usually about half a skink's length is made up of its long, pointy tail. Most skink tails are designed to snap off if pulled on hard, then wriggle about on their own for a few seconds. New tails do grow but don't grow back completely.

Verdict: basically **FACT**

You can get rid of leeches by burning them off

Like sucking the venom out of a snakebite (see pages 26-27), this was once a standard feature in movies. Almost any jungle scene would feature people having to wade through waist-deep water, then finding their legs were covered in leeches. The next steps were:

1. Light a match.
2. Touch it to the leech.
3. Listen to the sizzle.
4. Watch leech drop off.

Would this be a good idea in real life?

The truth is...

No, it wouldn't. First, what are you doing with matches, you dummy? You may well burn yourself and everyone knows it's really dangerous to play with fire. Second, the leech WILL let go — but it will also vomit into the cut it's made in your skin. This is likely to cause an infection.

The best way to get rid of a leech is to slide your fingernail under each of its three suckers, making it fall off.

Verdict:  PHONY

Dogs can smell fear

You most often hear this from someone who's not at all afraid of dogs. Usually they're saying it to someone who is afraid of dogs. But is it true, can dogs really smell fear?

⭐ The truth is...

Dogs have incredibly sensitive noses. They can smell the difference between every single human they've ever met (except for identical twins). They can smell cancer cells with more accuracy than million-dollar scanning machines. They can even smell tiny changes in the air when electricity is present. So it's really not surprising that dogs can also smell chemicals in your sweat, which are released when you're nervous or fearful!

FACT

Verdict:

⭐ 5 things you (probably) didn't know about LIONS

1 Lions often sleep for up to 20 hours a day!

2 They cannot roar until they're two years old — but once they can, it can be heard up to 5 miles (8 km) away.

3 Male lions are very lazy: females do 90% of the hunting.

4 No two male lions have the same pattern of whiskers on their muzzles.

5 Lions are lucky to live beyond 10 years in the wild.

Goldfish have a 3-second memory

Everyone — especially if they own a goldfish — loves this fact. It makes goldfish owners feel better about keeping their pet in a teeny-tiny tank that it takes only a matter of seconds to swim around.

The idea is that the goldfish never gets bored, because by the time he swims around his bowl the goldfish has forgotten that he's already seen the plastic castle 2,925 times in the last three hours and 15 minutes.

Do I know you from somewhere?

 But the truth is…

Goldfish actually have quite good memories (compared to other fish, anyway). They have been taught to push levers, fetch things and do various other tricks. They seem to be able to remember skills they've learned for anything up to a year.

Verdict:

Chameleons change color for camouflage

Everyone knows that chameleons can change color. People will tell you it's a defense technique, which allows the lizards to blend in with their background. They can match rocks, leaves, sand, and all sorts of other natural environments. But is this well-known fact actually true?

★ The fact is...

First of all, not all chameleons can change color. Some are very happy staying the same color all the time, thank you.

Secondly, the chameleons that can change color don't really do it for disguise. Sometimes they change to a darker color when they're cold, as this allows them to absorb more heat. But usually they change color according to their mood, because they're angry, scared, trying to attract a female, etc.

Verdict: **PHONY**

Female praying mantises bite off the heads of their mates

Presumably, if this myth is true, there aren't many second dates in the praying mantis world. For years a rumor has been going around that the female praying mantis bites off the male's head during mating.

Various reasons have been given for this unromantic approach to female/male relations:

- It provides the female with protein, which she needs for the reproductive process.
- Biting the male's head off stops him from leaving before the job is done.
- Having his head bitten off is a signal to the male to release his sperm.

★ The truth is...

Mating is a risky business for the male praying mantis, because the female does sometimes bite off his head — but only if she's hungry. It doesn't always happen, and certainly isn't for any of the reasons suggested above.

Verdict: FACT — but doesn't always happen

I'D NEVER HAVE KNOWN...

... that woodpeckers' brains are fitted with shock absorbers

A woodpecker's beak hits a tree with a force that is hundreds of times more powerful than a space rocket taking off. So how come their bird brains don't turn to jelly?

First, the woodpecker's brain is protected by soft, shock-absorbing material that absorbs much of the force. Second, every time it strikes a blow, a special muscle pulls its brain backwards to counteract the force.

Punxsutawney Phil can predict Spring

In North America on February 2, people hoping for spring anxiously await news of what a groundhog called Punxsutawney Phil is up to. Has Phil come out of his burrow as winter ends? And more importantly, has the cute little rodent spotted his own shadow and run back in?

If Phil does spot his own shadow and legs it back into his hole, the bad news is that there's at least six weeks of winter left. If he doesn't, spring is on its way.

How much notice should we take of Phil's predictions?

The truth is...

Take this with a little pinch of salt. Phil's supporters also claim that he's over a hundred years old (about 10 times as old as most other groundhogs), and is kept alive by a mysterious Groundhog elixir*.

However, groundhogs do emerge from their burrows when they sense changes in light and temperature. So if you see wild groundhogs appearing, spring may well be on its way.

Verdict: PHONY

*A life-extending potion.

WHEN ANIMALS TELL THE TIME

Some birds seem to be very good at telling the time.

Owners of parrots report that the birds appear to know exactly what time the cover should come off their cage in the morning, and what time it should go back on again at night.

In places where lawn sprinklers come on at the same time each day, flocks of birds arrive a few minutes beforehand, ready for their baths.

You can cure a beesting by squeezing out the stinger

The sound of bees bumbling around is one of the things that tell you it's summer. Most people are happy to hear them buzzing along, pollinating flowers, and generally having a very nice time.

Until a bee stings you, that is.

A beesting leaves a little venomous barb in your skin. Some people will tell you the best way to deal with a beesting is to squeeze it out, like a pimple.

★ The truth is...

Squeezing out the sting is a bad idea, as it may actually force *more* venom out of the sting and under your skin. The best way to get the sting out is to scrape it out immediately, using a credit card or something similar.

Verdict: _____ **PHONY** _____

Elephants are scared of mice

It's a nice idea: one of the world's biggest animals being scared of one of the world's smallest. And it's an idea that is explored in many children's cartoons and movies, too.

But can it be true?

No, I'm NOT getting out of your way.

⭐ The answer is...

Elephants don't really meet mice in the wild, although they do come across them in captivity. But elephants don't have very good eyesight, so they would be unlikely to even *notice* a mouse — let alone hurry away from it.

Verdict:

Camels store water in their humps

Camels are brilliantly adapted for life in the desert.
They have extra-wide feet, which helps them walk across loose
sand without sinking in. Their thick coats reflect sunlight
and keep out heat, but keep the camels warm at night. Their
mouths are able to chew thorny desert plants. And — best of all
— they can store water in their humps. Can't they?

The truth is...

Camels *are* brilliantly adapted for desert life*, and their humps
are one of these adaptations — but they don't contain water.
In fact, the hump contains fat. The camel stores fat in its hump
(instead of all over the body like humans do) so that there's no
layer of fat to trap heat in the high temperatures of the desert.

*For example, camels release so little moisture through their bodies that
camel pee is thick like syrup, and their poop is so dry you can set light to it!

Verdict: ―――― PHONY ――――

75

Hares go nuts in March

The idea of hares going nuts in March has become a saying that has little to do with animals. When someone's behaving oddly, rushing around and using loads of energy for no obvious reason, people say:

"He/she's mad as a March hare."

Apparently, in March hares start to race around, have boxing matches with other hares, suddenly jump straight up in the air, and generally behave strangely.

 And the truth is...

Hares are normally very shy, but during the spring mating season* they do start behaving differently. Their behavior seems nuts, but it isn't — not if you're a hare, and you're looking for love. The racing around, boxing, and jumping in the air are all mating behavior.

*Which is in March in northern Europe, where this phrase comes from.

Verdict: FACT

76

⭐5 things you (probably) didn't know about OCTOPUSES

1 Octopuses have three hearts.

2 An octopus weighing about the same as a 10-year-old can squeeze through a hole the size of a tennis ball.

3 An octopus's eyes have rectangular pupils (the black bits).

4 If a predator pulls off an octopus's arm, it can escape and re-grow another one later.

5 Octopuses can use their tentacles to open jam jars, or to hold stones like hammers for opening shellfish!

I'D NEVER HAVE KNOWN...

... that toads sometimes explode

It happened in Hamburg, Germany in 2005, during the toads' mating season. They suddenly began exploding for no obvious reason.

Eventually the cause was discovered. Crows had worked out how to peck out a toad's liver with one fast strike. The toads would puff themselves up to try and scare off the attackers, there would be an odd screeching sound as the toad's insides bulged through the pecked hole — and then they would explode! Yuck.

The strange case of the lovesick moose

There's something comical about a moose. Their big, gangly legs, thick bodies, oddly shaped faces, and antlers give them a slightly sad, "made-of-spare-parts" look. But this is the story of one especially comical moose: the moose that fell in love with a plastic deer.

The deer was set up in a backyard to be used as a target for archers. But one day in the mating season, a male moose wandered into the yard and took a shine to its plastic relative.

The moose paid *such* close attention to the plastic deer that its antlers fell off… soon followed by its head. At that point, the male moose lost interest and disappeared into the woods!

 And the truth is…

This story is almost certainly true: this kind of behavior isn't uncommon among desperate male animals. In the Año Nuevo elephant seal sanctuary in California, for example, males who have not found a mate head for Losers' Alley, where they snuggle up to logs as a substitute for female seals.

Verdict:

The tarantula is the world's deadliest spider

Anyone who's been stuck indoors watching TV on a rainy Sunday afternoon knows the scene: James Bond is asleep/in the shower/having a bath, and what do you see creeping up on him? A massive, hairy, deadly spider, put there by Bond's enemies to kill him. It's a tarantula!

But just how much danger is Bond *really* in?

★ The truth is...

There are actually lots of different kinds of tarantulas — and very few of them would be likely to do Bond much harm. No one is ever known to have died from a tarantula bite. A few tarantulas have a bite that can cause severe discomfort for a few days, but most are harmless to humans. The tarantula probably got its starring role because it was easily visible on screen.

The world's deadliest spider is actually the Brazilian wandering spider, which does sometimes kill humans.

Verdict: PHONY

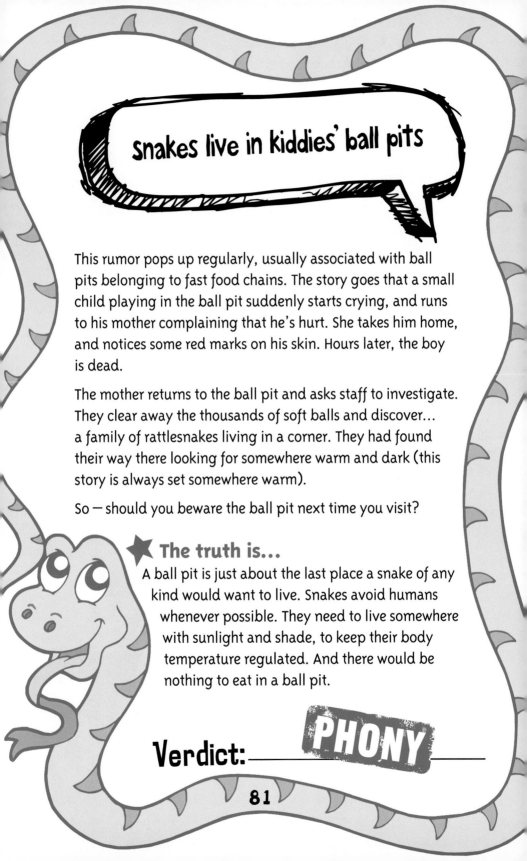

snakes live in kiddies' ball pits

This rumor pops up regularly, usually associated with ball pits belonging to fast food chains. The story goes that a small child playing in the ball pit suddenly starts crying, and runs to his mother complaining that he's hurt. She takes him home, and notices some red marks on his skin. Hours later, the boy is dead.

The mother returns to the ball pit and asks staff to investigate. They clear away the thousands of soft balls and discover… a family of rattlesnakes living in a corner. They had found their way there looking for somewhere warm and dark (this story is always set somewhere warm).

So — should you beware the ball pit next time you visit?

⭐ The truth is...

A ball pit is just about the last place a snake of any kind would want to live. Snakes avoid humans whenever possible. They need to live somewhere with sunlight and shade, to keep their body temperature regulated. And there would be nothing to eat in a ball pit.

Verdict: ─── PHONY ───

WHEN ANIMALS ATTACK!

ESCAPING A BULL

Halfway across a field, you suddenly become aware of a very large, angry-looking bull snorting at you.

How do you avoid being torn limb from limb?

⭐ *Stand still! Bulls can't see very well, and if you don't move, it will probably wander off.*

⭐ *If the bull does start to charge, run for it. Bulls can run faster than humans, so aim to get up a tree or behind something before the bull reaches you.*

⭐ *Throw things behind you — maybe a coat you were holding. The bull might stop and investigate it, giving you time to escape.*

Porcupines fire their quills at enemies

If you meet a porcupine while out for a walk one day, and it turns its back on you — watch out! It may be preparing to fire its quills at you. At least, that's what plenty of people think.

If true, this would mean porcupines have a brilliant defense system. But does it really exist?

 The truth is...

People who believe this myth usually come from places where porcupines don't live. A porcupine's quills are actually thick, stiff hairs. Imagine trying to fire your hair at people. It wouldn't work.

Porcupines do have a great defense system, though. The quills have barbed ends. If an animal tries to bite the porcupine it turns round. The attacker gets a face full of quills, which are not fired but break off. The quills hook into the flesh and often become infected.

Verdict:

I'D NEVER HAVE KNOWN...

... that walruses are right-handed

Of course, I play the guitar with my <u>other</u> hand.

Walruses just love to eat clams, which live buried in the seabed. They like them so much that a walrus can pack away over 6,000 juicy clams in one meal.

To expose the clams, walruses fan away the surrounding material using their front flipper. And they almost always use the right flipper to do this, very rarely the left.

Poodles sometimes go "baa!"

In 2007, Internet sites, email circulars and the newspapers were suddenly full of the most amazing story from Japan.

Apparently, dog lovers who had always wanted a poodle had been delighted to find somewhere selling them for half the usual price — only to realize later that there was something very different about these "poodles." They *did* have the fancy pom-pom haircut that poodles often have. But they wouldn't bark, sit, lie down, fetch a ball, or do any of the other things dogs normally find exciting.

The strange poodles kept growing and growing, and eventually stopped looking like poodles at all. In fact, they started to look like what they were — sheep.

A dishonest businessman had been giving lambs a poodle haircut, then selling them to dog-loving people in Japan. Because sheep are rare in Japan, people often didn't spot the difference.

 The truth is...

This is a 100% made-up story, which first appeared on the Internet. It's also very insulting to Japanese people, who would have to be pretty dumb not to spot the difference between a puppy and a lamb, however cute they both are!

Verdict: — **PHONY** —

SNAKES HAVE BEEN

Some people love animals so much, they'll do almost anything to spend time with them. They'll let their dog sleep on the bed, spend a fortune on expensive cat food, or take their pet lobster with them when they go for a walk (see page 20).

There are even a few people who will take their pet snake along to a robbery...

CASE 1: THE BMX BANDIT

A teenager was spotted trying to steal a flashlight from a hardware store in California. When the staff tried to stop him, he revealed the snake wrapped around his arm. Everyone jumped backwards, and the pesky young thief pedaled off on his bike.

CASE 2: SNAKE NOT-SO-CHARMING

In the Indian capital Delhi, tourists enjoy watching snake charmers. What they're not so excited about is being robbed at snakepoint. Snakes have been used in several crimes in the city. One of the most frightening was when two men coiled a constrictor around a businessman's neck. They refused to remove it until he gave them money.

USED IN STICKUPS

Two people were walking along the streets of New Jersey one evening when a car screeched to a stop beside them. A man leaped out and brandished a snake, while two more men got out of the car and went through the walkers' pockets.

⭐ And the truth is...

These are all real cases — and there have been plenty of others, too. Using a snake as a deadly weapon seems to be on the increase!

Verdict: FACT

OTHER (TRUE) STORIES ABOUT SNAKES:

1. Dead rattlesnakes can still bite you a day later!

2. Black mambas are not black. They're grey, brown, or olive colored.

3. Seven of the 10 deadliest types of snake live in Australia.

4. Snakes are sometimes born with two heads. The heads of a two-headed snake will fight each other for food, even though they share the same stomach.

WHEN ANIMALS ATTACK!

ESCAPING KILLER BEES

Killer bees are just like ordinary bees — except much more aggressive. When disturbed, they will pour out of their hive and chase away their target. If you meet these buzzing terrors...

DO

 Run like crazy — the bees sometimes chase their victims for hundreds of yards before giving up.

 Wrap something around your face to stop your eyes from being stung (but make sure you can still see where you're going!)

DON'T

 Dive into water — the bees will just wait for you to surface.

 Wave your hands and arms — bees are attracted to movement.

Vultures attack live victims

Imagine the scene...

You're lost in the desert (perhaps your sand-boarding expedition has gone back to the hotel without you). You've been out there in the heat for a long time, and your strength is failing. Then you see something you've been dreading: vultures, circling!!

You sit to rest in the shade of a rock, and a vulture lands nearby. Its bare neck and head look evil. You know vultures are featherless so that the birds can more easily stick their heads inside dead creatures. Another vulture lands, and another. They start to hop closer, then to peck at your feet.

Are you about to be become lunch for a wake* of vultures — while you're still alive?

 The truth is...

It could happen, though you'd have to be very weak — too weak to move, probably. Vultures prefer their food to be dead, but they do occasionally attack dying prey.

* "Wake" is the word for a group of feeding vultures. Circling vultures are often called a "kettle." A group in a tree is called a "committee," "venue," or "volt."

FACT

Verdict:

89

Female black widow spiders kill their mate

It's not much of a life being a male black widow spider. You'll only live about six weeks, compared to a female's three years. Your venom sacs stopped developing as you reached adulthood, so you can't take out your annoyance by poisoning something. As an adult you don't get to eat anything (which is why those sacs have become useless). Instead you have to spend all your time searching for a mate.

And then, to cap it all, when you *do* find a mate, she's quite likely to get annoyed with you almost immediately. She'll bite your head off — literally — if you're not very, very careful.

 The truth is...

This is all true — although how often a female black widow bites off a male's head is not certain. It happens in captivity, but very rarely in the wild.

Verdict: **FACT** (just about)

WHEN ANIMALS TELL THE TIME

In South Africa, the local baboons love to break open people's garbage bins and see if there are any tasty leftovers inside.

Amazingly, they seem to know which day of the week the garbage is put out. They arrive early in the morning, and wait for the bins to be put out — ready to rummage for a free meal.

Chocolate is poisonous to dogs

This is a myth that doesn't really seem to make sense. After all, dogs are very like humans — that's why animal-testing laboratories test products on dogs before approving them for human consumption. If *we* can eat chocolate, surely dogs must be able to as well? Especially as they seem to like it so much...

★ The truth is...

Chocolate contains a chemical called theobromine, which in dogs causes muscle tremors, seizures, or even heart attacks. So it is poisonous to dogs, who don't have to eat very much of it to get sick or die.

Verdict: ——— FACT ———

Other things (truly) poisonous to dogs:

It's not only chocolate! You also need to make sure dogs don't chow down:

1. Grapes and raisins

2. Onions

3. Macadamia nuts

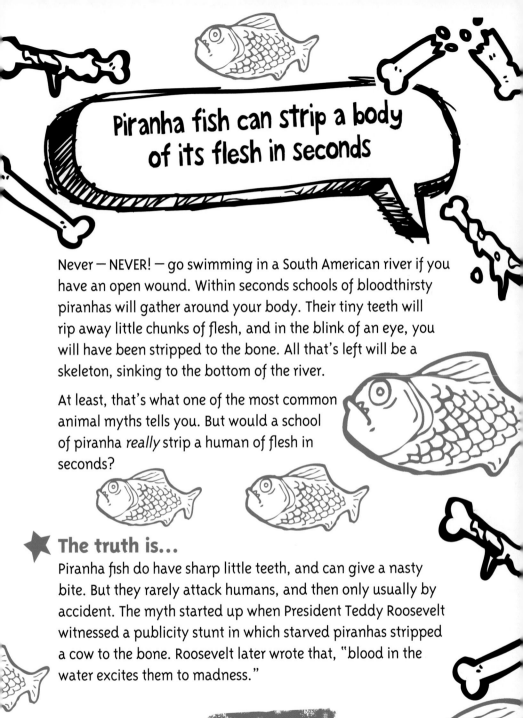

Piranha fish can strip a body of its flesh in seconds

Never — NEVER! — go swimming in a South American river if you have an open wound. Within seconds schools of bloodthirsty piranhas will gather around your body. Their tiny teeth will rip away little chunks of flesh, and in the blink of an eye, you will have been stripped to the bone. All that's left will be a skeleton, sinking to the bottom of the river.

At least, that's what one of the most common animal myths tells you. But would a school of piranha *really* strip a human of flesh in seconds?

★ The truth is...

Piranha fish do have sharp little teeth, and can give a nasty bite. But they rarely attack humans, and then only usually by accident. The myth started up when President Teddy Roosevelt witnessed a publicity stunt in which starved piranhas stripped a cow to the bone. Roosevelt later wrote that, "blood in the water excites them to madness."

Verdict: —— PHONY ——

GLOSSARY

adrenaline a hormone commonly used in describing the symptoms such as increased heart rate and breathing that occur in response to stress and the feelings of heightened energy, danger, fright, excitement, and alertness

aggressive acting with forceful energy and purpose, or showing a readiness to attack

assert to say in a strong and definite way

captivity the state of being caged

circulate to pass from person to person or place to place, or to become well-known or widespread

debris the remains of something that has been broken

domesticated bred and raised for use by people

expedition a trip made for a certain purpose

infectious capable of causing the spread of germs inside the body, causing illness

lurk to lie in wait or move in stealth, especially for an evil purpose

malaria a human disease in red blood cells, transmitted by tcharacterized by recurring attacks of chills and fever

matador a bullfighter

maul to injure by or as if by beating

pedigree the recorded purity of breed of an individual animal

ruminant hoofed mammal that chews mainly grass, and has several chambers in its stomach

rummage to make a thorough search or investigation

seabed the floor of a sea or ocean

seizure a sudden attack resulting from abnormal electrical discharges in the brain

skink small lizards with long tapering bodies that eat insects

tentacle a long, thin body part that sticks out from an animal's head or mouth

tourniquet a device (such as a band of rubber) that checks bleeding or blood flow by compressing blood vessels

trance a sleeplike state (such as deep hypnosis) usually characterized by lack of movement and lowered senses and motor activity

twitch to move or pull with a sudden motion

venom something an animal makes in its body that can harm other animals

venomous able to produce a liquid called venom that is harmful to other animals

FOR MORE INFORMATION

BOOKS

Grubman, Steve. *Orangutans Are Ticklish: Fun Facts from an Animal Photographer*. New York: Schwartz & Wade Books, 2010.

Loy, Jessica. *Weird and Wild Animal Facts*. New York: Henry Holt and Company, 2010.

Scientific American. *Fact or Fiction: Science Tackles 58 Popular Myths*. New York: Scientific American, 2013.

WEBSITES

Animal Myths Busted
http://kids.nationalgeographic.com/explore/nature/animal-myths-busted/#myths-toad.jpg

9 Myths About Animals You Probably Think Are True
http://www.sierraclub.org/sierra/2015-2-march-april/green-life/9-myths-about-animals-you-probably-think-are-true

Animal Facts
http://www.sciencekids.co.nz/sciencefacts/animals.html

Publisher's note to educators and parents: Our editors have carefully reviewed these websites to ensure that they are suitable for students. Many websites change frequently, however, and we cannot guarantee that a site's future contents will continue to meet our high standards of quality and educational value. Be advised that students should be closely supervised whenever they access the Internet.

Where can I find myths about...